The Quick & Easy Mediterranean Diet Cookbook

"Delicious Mediterranean Diet Recipes Which Can Be Made In Minutes"

Disclaimer

All rights reserved. No part of this Book may be reproduced, stored in a retrieval system, or transmitted, in any form, or by any means, including mechanical or electronic, without the prior written permission of the author, nor be otherwise circulated in any form.

While the author has made every effort to ensure that the ideas, guidelines and information presented in this Book are safe, they should be used at the reader's discretion. The author cannot be held responsible for any personal or commercial damage arising from the application or misinterpretation of information presented herein.

Contents

Disclaimer 2
Introduction 6
About Mediterranean Diet 8
Mediterranean Diet Recipes 13

    Walnut and Cranberry Canapés 13

    Olive Eggplant Dip served with Bell Peppers 15

    Seafood Stew 18

    Baked Red Snapper with Olives and Tomatoes .. 21

    Fennel Salad with Vegetables, Eggs and Tuna 23

    Turkey Cutlets in a Caper Sauce 27

    Grilled Vegetable Tagine served over Couscous ... 30

    Chicken over Sun-Dried Tomato Orzo 33

    Meat Loaves with Arugula Salad 37

    Spice rubbed Grilled Steak & Sweet Potatoes 40

    Hot Cinnamon Breakfast Couscous 42

    Mediterranean Edamame Stew 44

    Gnocchi with Pancetta & Peppery Watercress ... 46

    Homemade Pizza with Tomatoes & Pesto 49

    Baked Roasted Green Peppers 51

Crisp Lettuce Wraps with Red Pepper Hummus 53

Halibut Grill with Skordalia 56

Authentic Middle Eastern Chicken Shawarma 60

Luscious Fish with Lemon-Fennel Salad 63

Stuffed Portobello Mushrooms 66

Seasoned Beef Patties and Cucumber Salad 70

Turkey with Honeyed Grapefruit Relish 73

Spicy Chicken Thighs in Brussels sprouts 76

Lemon-Mint Parsley Tabbouleh 79

Herb Crusted Lamb Chops with Couscous Salad 82

Grouper Fillets in a Tomato-Caper Sauce 85

Sautéed Vegetable Calzone 88

Savory Poached Pears 91

Icy Almond Date Yoghurt Shake 93

Braised Garlic Kale with Cherry Tomatoes 95

Traditional Lentil & Bulgur Pilaf with Squash 97

Beef Rice Bake with Mushrooms & Cranberries 100

Purple Cabbage and Sunflower Butter Soup 104

Basil walnut Pesto Spread 107

Conclusion 109

Introduction

This recipe book offers 35 mouth-watering dishes that evoke the essence of the Mediterranean region. These recipes are not only easy to prepare but super delicious to taste bursting with intense flavour that is sure to please your entire family. The best part is each recipe can be prepared in less than 30 minutes. With a special emphasis on healthy ingredients like legumes, lean meats, whole grains, veggies and fruits, these recipes have been carefully selected for today's busy lifestyle.

There are classic favourites like chicken shawarma, lettuce wraps with red pepper hummus, lentil & bulgur pilaf, fish with lemon-fennel salad and roasted green peppers.

The cinnamon couscous is an excellent breakfast with cinnamon in it to add a unique flavour. There are spicy chicken thighs nestled in Brussel sprouts. We have got canapés which has a great combination walnut, goat cheese and cranberry. Purple cabbage soup is a nutritious bright coloured soup with sunflower seed butter. Try savoury poached pears prepared in a traditional style for weeknight desserts.

Rich in healthy nutrients but low in cholesterol and fats, these intensely flavoured recipes are nourishment for your body, soul and mind. Apart from the benefits you'll find a simplified approach to Mediterranean cooking. This book will give you a great dining experience.

About Mediterranean Diet

The Mediterranean diet is the staple diet of people living on the shores of the Mediterranean sea- Spain, Syria, Italy, Morocco, France, Turkey, Greece Lebanon, Israel and the Middle East. Mediterranean cuisine is vibrant and colorful because of the rich cultural heritage of diverse countries. The Mediterranean diet is a good option for people who are looking for a heart-healthy diet plan. Apart from following the basic healthy diet plan, the Mediterranean diet is made in a traditional way and involves usage of red wine and flavorful olive oil. Other key components include protein-rich legumes, whole grains, low fat dairy products and fish.

Key Components of the Mediterranean diet

1. **Switch to veggies and fruits and whole grains.** The diet includes mainly plant-based foods, whole grains, legumes and nuts, vegetables and fruits. Include food that is unprocessed or minimally processed. Fresh fruits, vegetables, whole grain bread, baby carrots, cereal and whole grain rice are best for this type of diet.
2. **Healthy Nuts**- Choose nuts in your snack for a good source of protein and fiber. Cashews, almonds, walnuts and pistachios are good options. Natural peanut butter and

sesame seeds are used a spread or dip for snacks.

3. **Low-fat dairy products.** Low fat cheese, Fat free yoghurt and skimmed milk are mainly used in all the recipes. Use of ice cream and whole milk is highly limited.

4. **Spice it up.** Use of salt is limited. Herbs and spices are used to flavor foods instead of salts.

5. **Go fish.** Fish is the main ingredient as the people live around sea shore. The diet includes having fish 2-3 times a week. Some of the choices include trout, tuna, mackerel, herring and salmon. There are different ways to eat these fish. You can broil, bake or grill instead of frying the fish.

6. **Say no to butter:** Canola oil and olive oil is a healthy choice over unhealthy butter. Olive oil has healthy fats. There is flavorful olive oil available in the market. Just drizzle over your vegetables or add a touch of flavorful oil for a unique flavor.

7. **Cut on the red meat:** Eat red meat once or twice in a month. Always choose lean meat and keep the quantity as low as possible. Avoid processed high fat meats like bacon and sausage.

8. **A moderate amount of wine:** It is a known fact that a moderate amount of wine is good for health as it reduces the risk of

heart disease. Women and men can have 5 ounces of red wine daily. Do not drink more than 10 ounces otherwise it might give invitation to some health problems including cancer.

Benefits of the Mediterranean diet

1. **Heart Disease and Stroke:** Reduced risk of heart disease and stroke.

2. **Life expectancy**: The diet prevents a number of diseases, thus increasing the overall life expectancy.

3. **High Cholesterol:** The diet help lowering the cholesterol level.

4. **High Blood Pressure**: As the diet includes low sodium ingredients, it helps in the prevention of hypertension.

5. **Weight Loss:** Low fat and fat free ingredients helps losing weight safely.

6. **Cancer:** Consuming low fat dairy products decreases the risk of prostate cancer.

7. **Diabetes**: Mediterranean diet has limited use of salt and sugar, thus helps prevent type 2 Diabetes.

8. **Osteoporosis:** Some studies have confirmed that people eating a mediterranean diet have lower rates of bone fractures.

9. **Alzheimer's disease:** Fresh fruits and vegetables have antioxidants that prevent Alzheimer's disease.

10. **Other diseases**: This diet helps alleviating constipation, autoimmune diseases, arthritis irritable bowel syndrome and blindness.

Mediterranean Diet Recipes

Walnut and Cranberry Canapés

A great combination of flavors of walnut, goat cheese and cranberry in canapés

Serves 8

Cooking Time 20 minutes

Nutritional Information: Calories 275, Total Fat 15g, Protein 11g, Carbohydrates 26g, Dietary Fiber 1.2g

Ingredients

Dried cranberries-1/2 cup

Goat cheese-8 ounces

Whole-wheat baguette-1/2

Ground cinnamon-1/8 teaspoon

Olive oil-4 teaspoons

22 walnut halves-3/4 cup

Fresh thyme leaves for garnishing

Salt and pepper

Fresh thyme, chopped -1 teaspoon

Cooking Method

1. Take half whole wheat baguette and cut 22 thin slices. Prepare oven to 375 degrees. Take cinnamon and one teaspoon of oil on a rimmed baking sheet and toss walnuts in it. Now season with pepper & salt.
2. Bake for six minutes until it turns golden. Spread slices of baguette on the same sheet and brush over with olive oil. Season again with some pepper and salt.
3. Bake for ten more minutes until toasted. Keep aside and let cool.
4. Mix cheese with two tablespoon water in a bowl to form a smooth mixture. Add thyme and cranberries. Season with pepper and salt.
5. Spread this mixture evenly on baguette slices. Place a walnut on the top of each slices and garnish with thyme leaves.

Olive Eggplant Dip served with Bell Peppers

A Middle Eastern dip made with roasted eggplant with olives, garlic and spices

Serves 4

Cooking Time 25 minutes

Nutritional Information: Calories 68, Total Fat 5.6g, Protein 1.3g, Carbohydrates 4.3g, Dietary Fiber 2.1g

Ingredients

2 yellow bell peppers

Italian eggplants, halved- 2 (10 ounces each)

Olive oil-1 1/2 teaspoons

1 garlic clove, sliced

Coarse salt-1/4 teaspoon

Kalamata olives, pitted -1/2 cup

Green olives, pitted -1/2 cup

Fresh oregano, finely chopped -1 teaspoon

Oregano leaves for garnish

Lemon zest, finely grated -1 teaspoon

Pinch of red-pepper flakes

Cooking Method

1. Remove the ribs and seeds of yellow bell pepper and cut it into one and a half inch pieces. Preheat oven to 400 degrees. Brush oil on a rimmed baking sheet.
2. Arrange eggplants on the sheet with the cut sides facing up. Sprinkle garlic and salt over eggplants. Roast for twenty minutes until it turns soft and golden. Keep aside to cool.
3. Now carefully take out flesh and separate its seeds. Transfer the garlic and the seedless flesh into a processor and process. Transfer the puree to a bowl.
4. Similarly process olives in the processor and process for 1-2 seconds until coarsely chopped. Transfer chopped olives into the bowl of eggplant puree.
5. To the bowl add red pepper flakes, oil, lemon zest and chopped oregano.
6. Garnish with lemon zest and extra oregano leaves. Serve immediately with yellow bell peppers.

Seafood Stew

Treat yourself to this delicious seafood stew that features red snapper, clams and scallops

Serves 4

Cooking Time 25 minutes

Nutritional Information: Calories 410, Total Fat 7.8g, Protein 41g, Carbohydrates 28g, Dietary Fiber 3 g

Ingredients

Scallops, muscle removed- 8

Clams, cleaned and scrubbed-8

Red snapper fillet, skinless - 1/2 pound

Clam juice- One 8-ounce

Dry white wine-1/2 cup

Orange zest, finely grated -1/2 teaspoon

Olive oil-1 tablespoon

Fresh oregano, roughly chopped -2 tablespoons

1 jalapeno pepper, thinly sliced into rounds

Lime juice-1 tablespoon

Brown olives-1/3 cup pitted

1 yellow onion

2 garlic cloves, minced

1 tomato

Water-1 cup

Low-sodium chicken broth-1 cup

Parsley leaves for garnishing

Cooking Method

1. Cut the snapper fillet into two inch pieces, tomato into half inch wedges and onion into ¼ inch slices.
2. Heat oil in a saucepan over medium heat and add onion slices. Sauté for a couple of minutes until it turns golden brown.
3. Add garlic, brown olives, oregano, lime juice, and jalapeno to the saucepan and cook for few minutes. Add in orange zest and wine; cook for 3-4 minutes until the cooking juice is reduced to half.
4. Stir in chicken broth, tomato, water and clam juice and boil. Reduce the heat to low and stir in snapper, clams and scallops.
5. Cover with a lid and let it simmer for 10-15 minutes. The scallops and snapper will turn opaque in the center and clams will open up. Throw away unopened clams.
6. Top with parsley leaves and serve into bowls.

Baked Red Snapper with Olives and Tomatoes

A highly flavored baked fish recipe with the combination of tomatoes, thyme and olives

Serves 4

Cooking Time 30 minutes

Nutritional Information: Calories 395, Total Fat 21g, Protein 40g, Carbohydrates 7g, Dietary Fiber 1g

Ingredients

Red snapper fillets-2 (6 ounce)

Kalamata olives, pitted & halved-10

Olive oil-2 tablespoons

3 plum tomatoes

1 shallot

Fresh thyme, chopped-2 teaspoons

Cooked white rice

Aluminium foil- 18 inches long

Cooking Method

1. Chop plum tomatoes, thyme and shallot; mix everything in a bowl. Season with pepper and salt. Keep aside
2. Brush oil on an aluminium foil and arrange snapper fillets on it.
3. Spread tomato mixture on top of the fillets. Sprinkle with pitted olives on tomato mixture. Drizzle fillets with olive oil.
4. Fold the aluminium foil over to enclose the content and crimp foil edges to seal.
5. Heat a baking sheet in a preheated oven (450 F) for ten minutes. Place the aluminium foil packet with the fish inside on this baking sheet.
6. Bake for 12 minutes until fish is opaque in the center. Open the foil after 5 minutes and serve over rice.

Fennel Salad with Vegetables, Eggs and Tuna

An authentic mediterranean salad of sliced vegetables, eggs and tuna arranged in an overlapping pattern

Serves 3

Cooking Time 20 minutes

Nutritional Information: Calories 270, Total Fat 21g, Protein 13g, Carbohydrates 9g, Dietary Fiber 2g

Ingredients

Dressing

Lemon zest-1 tsp

Lemon juice-1 Tbsp

Olive oil-4 tbsp

Freshly ground black pepper

Salt

Fennel greens, chopped -1 tsp

Salad

Capers-1 Tbsp

Tuna, drained-1 can

2 hard-cooked eggs, quartered

12 black and green olives

Radishes-8

Red onion, sliced-1

Fennel bulbs -2 small

White wine vinegar

Yellow bell pepper, sliced-1

Cooking Method

1. For the dressing: Combine together lemon juice, salt, pepper, oil and lemon zest in a bowl. Refrigerate for few hours for better results.
2. Chop the fennel greens and add this to salad dressing.
3. For the salad: Trim the fennel bulbs and cut thin slices lengthwise. Add vinegar to onion slices; toss and keep aside for few minutes until they turn bright.
4. Take a large salad plate and place pepper rings first. Then arrange sliced fennel on top of the pepper rings. Use your creativity and arrange radishes and olives.
5. Place the fish in the center of the salad and eggs in clusters.
6. Scatter 1 tablespoon of capers over fish. Drain the onions slices and arrange them over your salad set them. Pour the dressing all over the salad. Season with pepper and salt.
7. Serve immediately.

Turkey Cutlets in a Caper Sauce

Turkey cutlets served in a flavorful lemon and caper sauce

Serves 4

Cooking Time 30 minutes

Nutritional Information: Calories 301, Total Fat 11g, Protein 35g, Carbohydrates 8g, Dietary Fiber 1g

Ingredients

Reduced-sodium chicken broth- 1 can

Dry white wine-1/2 can

Drained capers, chopped-2 Tbsp

All-purpose flour-¼ cup

4 Turkey breast cutlets, halved crosswise - 1¼ lb

Egg-1

Olive oil-1/2 cup

Lemon slices -8

Unsalted butter-1 Tbsp

Cooking Method

1. On a plate mix one fourth tablespoon of pepper and salt with all purpose flour.
2. In a small bowl take one tablespoon of water and egg and whisk vigorously with a fork.
3. Roll turkey pieces in the seasoned flour until well coated. Shake off excess flour.
4. Meanwhile heat olive oil in a skillet over medium heat. Dip the turkey pieces in the egg mixture and drop into the skillet.
5. Cook for 8-10 minutes until browned. Turn and brown the other side too. Place the turkey cutlets on paper towels to remove excess oil.
6. Heat 1 tablespoon of oil in a medium saucepan and stir in capers and lemon slices Cook for 3 minutes until golden brown.
7. Transfer lemon and onto a plate.
8. Stir in broth and wine; let simmer for 5 minutes until thickened. Put turkey cutlets to saucepan and add butter.
9. Cover and let simmer for 6 more minutes until turkey is fully cooked. Garnish with slices of lemon.

Grilled Vegetable Tagine served over Couscous

Mediterranean tagine of vegetables served with grilled onions and peppers over couscous

Serves 4

Cooking Time 30 minutes

Nutritional Information: Calories 461, Total Fat 7g, Protein 14.7g, Carbohydrates 94.3g, Dietary Fiber 13g

Ingredients

Red onion-1

Red bell pepper, cut into quarters-2

Green bell pepper, cut into quarters-1

Balsamic vinegar-2 teaspoons

Kosher salt, divided-1/2 teaspoon

Olive oil, divided-1 teaspoon

Chopped onion-1 3/4 cups

2 garlic cloves, minced

Ground cumin-1 teaspoon

Crushed fennel seeds-1/2 teaspoon

Ground cinnamon-1/4 teaspoon

Water, divided-1 1/4 cups

Pitted green olives, sliced -1/4 cup

Golden raisins-1/4 cup

Freshly ground black pepper

Tomatoes, diced -1 (28-ounce) can

6 red potatoes, quartered

Cooking spray

Uncooked couscous-2/3 cup

Toasted pine nuts-1/4 cup

Cooking Method

1. Prepare grill coated with cooking spray.
2. Cut onion into four wedges and leave the root end intact. Now combine half teaspoon of oil, one fourth teaspoon of salt, vinegar, bell peppers and red onion slices in a medium bowl.
3. Heat oil in a nonstick saucepan over medium heat. Stir in garlic and chopped onion and sauté for 2 minutes.
4. Stir in fennel seeds, ground cinnamon and cumin and sauté for 30 seconds.
5. Add potatoes, tomatoes, olives and cook for 4 minutes. Add one fourth cup water, raisin, salt and black pepper and boil.
6. Reduce the heat; cover and let simmer for 20 minutes until vegetables are tender.
7. Place out onion and bell peppers on the prepared grill and grill both sides for 8 minutes
8. In a small saucepan boil one cup water and stir in couscous gradually. Let stand for five minutes.

9. Serve vegetable mixture over the hot couscous and place grilled onion, peppers and toasted pine nuts on top.

Chicken over Sun-Dried Tomato Orzo

A hearty weeknight dinner made with sun dried tomatoes, orzo and luscious chicken

Serves 4

Cooking Time 30 minutes

Nutritional Information: Calories 457, Total Fat 12g, Protein 36g, Carbohydrates 54g, Dietary Fiber 10g

Ingredients

Romano cheese, finely shredded -1/2 cup

Artichoke hearts, frozen & thawed-1 9-ounce package

4 chicken breasts-1 1/4 pound

Red-wine vinegar-1 tablespoon

Chopped marjoram, divided-3 teaspoons

1 clove garlic, peeled

1 plum tomato, diced

Whole wheat orzo-8 ounces

Sun-dried tomatoes, chopped -1/2 cup

Salt-1/4 teaspoon

Freshly ground pepper-1/4 teaspoon

Extra-virgin olive oil-3 teaspoons

Cooking Method

1. Bring water to a boil in a saucepan and cook orzo according to directions on package for ten minutes until it turns tender. Drain and keep aside.
2. Combine plum tomatoes, one-fourth cup sun dried tomatoes, vinegar, oil, garlic, marjoram and one cup water in a blender and blend roughly.
3. Marinate chicken in pepper and salt. Heat 1 tablespoon olive oil in a skillet over high heat. Reduce the heat to medium and add in chicken and cook for 5 minutes until both sides are golden brown. Transfer chicken on paper towels.
4. Transfer the tomato sauce to a pan and boil. Take out half cup sauce and keep in a small bowl. To the pan add one fourth cup sun dried tomatoes. Add orzo, six tablespoon cheese and artichoke hearts; cook for 2 minutes until heated. Divide this mixture into 4 servings.
5. Cut the chicken into slices. Top each serving of orzo with chicken slices, tomato sauce, cheese and marjoram.

Meat Loaves with Arugula Salad

Delicious meat loves topped with yoghurt sauce and serves with arugula, cucumber salad

Serves 4

Cooking Time 20 minutes

Nutritional Information: Calories 345 ,Total Fat 15.4g, Protein 32g, Carbohydrates 12g, Dietary Fiber 1.5g

Ingredients

Lean ground lamb-5 ounces

Ground sirloin -10 ounce

Red onion, grated -1/3 cup

Dry breadcrumbs-1/3 cup

Fresh thyme, chopped -4 teaspoons

Fresh mint, chopped -4 teaspoons

Salt, divided-3/8 teaspoon

Red pepper flakes, crushed -1/4 teaspoon

Ground allspice-1/4 teaspoon

3 garlic cloves, minced

1 large egg, lightly beaten

Cooking spray

Lemon juice, divided-2 tablespoons

Fat-free Greek yogurt -1/2 cup

Extra-virgin olive oil-1 tablespoon

Reduced-fat feta, crumbled-2 ounces

Freshly ground black pepper-1/4 teaspoon

Cucumber, 1/4-inch-thick slices- 1 1/2 cups

Baby arugula leaves-4 cups

Cooking Method

1. Preheat oven to 450°.
2. In a bowl combine sirloin, lamb, breadcrumbs and red onion. Add in salt, allspice, one tablespoon of mint and thyme. Stir in red pepper flakes, cloves and beaten eggs; mix well.
3. Coat eight muffin cups with cooking oil. Transfer the meat mixture into these 8 cups and bake for 8 minutes at 450°.
4. Turn the broiler to high and broil for 3 minutes.
5. In a food processor, process feta, yoghurt, yogurt, feta, one teaspoon of lemon juice, thyme and mint.
6. For arugula salad- In a small bowl, combine salt, pepper, oil and remaining lemon juice. Stir in cucumber and arugula; toss well.
7. Serve meat loves topped with yoghurt sauce and arugula salad.

Spice rubbed Grilled Steak & Sweet Potatoes

Six fragrant spices give an aromatic flavor to these grilled steaks

Serves 2

Cooking Time 30 minutes

Nutritional Information: Calories 364, Total Fat 15g, Protein 33g, Carbohydrates 21g, Dietary Fiber 3g

Ingredients

1 red onion

1 sweet potato

8 ounces strip steak, cut into 2 portions

Cayenne pepper-1/4 teaspoon

Ground coriander-1/4 teaspoon

Ground ginger-1/2 teaspoon

Ground cinnamon-1/4 teaspoon

Ground cumin-1/2 teaspoon

Ground allspice-1/2 teaspoon

Orange zest, freshly grated -1/2 teaspoon

Cooking Method

1. Preheat grill to high. Cut onion and potato into thin slices. In a bowl, combine cumin, salt, allspice, cayenne, coriander, cinnamon and ginger. Use 3 teaspoons of this mixture to marinate steaks.
2. To the remaining spice in the bowl, add onion and sweet potatoes along with orange zest and oil. Toss well to coat
3. Take 2 24-inch aluminium foils and place one above the other. Coat the foil with cooking spray. Place the potato and onion mixture in the center and spread evenly making a thin layer. Seal the foil after folding it over.
4. Now put this packet in the preheated grill and cook for 6-7 minutes. After 6 minutes, turn it once and cook the other side too for 6-7 minutes.
5. Similarly grill both sides of the steak for 4-5 minutes each. Open up the aluminium packets and serve on a plate along with grilled steak.

Hot Cinnamon Breakfast Couscous

Let's get mediterranean with this quick & healthy cinnamon couscous for breakfast

Servings 4

Cooking Time 10 minutes

Nutritional Information: Calories 300, Total Fat 6g, Protein 12g, Carbohydrates 50g, Dietary Fiber 5g

Ingredients

Butter-4 teaspoons

Dark brown sugar- 6 teaspoons

Dried currants-1/4 cup

Dried apricots, chopped -1/2 cup

1% low-fat milk-3 cups

Whole-wheat uncooked couscous-1 cup

Cinnamon stick-1 (2-inch)

Salt-1/4 teaspoon

Cooking Method

1. Pour milk in a medium saucepan and add cinnamon stick. Heat the milk for 3 minutes over medium heat. Turn the heat off before reaching the boiling point.
2. Add in four teaspoons of brown sugar, salt, couscous, currants and apricots to the milk.
3. Cover the saucepan and leave the mixture undisturbed for 10-12 minutes. Discard cinnamon.
4. Spoon couscous into 4 serving bowls and top with butter and brown sugar. Serve immediately.

Mediterranean Edamame Stew

Quick and easy highly seasoned stew made with edamame and zucchini and tomatoes

Serves 4

Cooking Time 30 minutes

Nutritional Information: Calories 257, Total Fat 8g, Protein 15g, Carbohydrates 28g, Dietary Fiber 10g

Ingredients

Diced tomatoes-1 28-ounce can

Cayenne pepper-1/8 teaspoon

Frozen shelled edamame, thawed-3 cups

Ground coriander-1 teaspoon

Ground cumin-2 teaspoons

1 zucchini, diced

Extra-virgin olive oil-1 tablespoon

Minced garlic-2 tablespoons

Lemon juice-3 tablespoons

1 onion, chopped

Chopped cilantro-1/4 cup

Cooking Method

1. Boil water in a medium saucepan. Stir in edamame. Cook for 6-7 minutes until tender. Drain and keep aside.
2. Take olive oil in a skillet and heat over high heat. Stir in chopped onion and sauté for 3 minutes until soft and brown.
3. Stir in zucchini; cover and cook for another 4 minutes. Add cumin, cayenne, coriander and garlic; cook for 1 minute until fragrant.
4. Add diced tomatoes and cook for another 3-4 minutes. Cover, reduce the heat and let simmer until cooking juice is reduced.
5. Add in cooked edamame and cook for 1 minute. Spoon edamame on a serving plate and garnish with chopped cilantro and lemon juice.

Gnocchi with Pancetta & Peppery Watercress

Easy yet delicious combination of Italian pancetta, peppery watercress and gnocchi

Serves 4

Cooking Time 30minutes

Nutritional Information: Calories 370,Total Fat 7.5g, Protein 14.2g, Carbohydrates 62g, Dietary Fiber 3g

Ingredients

Watercress-4 ounces

Gnocchi-1 pound

Pancetta, chopped-2 ounces

Red-wine vinegar-2 teaspoons

Red pepper, crushed -1/4 teaspoon

2 large tomatoes, chopped

3 cloves garlic, minced

Sugar-1/2 teaspoon

Salt-1/4 teaspoon

Parmesan cheese, freshly grated -1/3 cup

Cooking Method

1. Cut the stems of the watercress and chop it coarsely. Add pancetta to a nonstick pan and cook for 6 minutes; keep stirring until browned. Add garlic and sauté for 1 minute.
2. Stir in tomatoes, red pepper and sugar and cook for 4 minutes until juicy. Add salt and vinegar
3. Bring water in a pan to boil.
4. Stir in gnocchi and cook for 4 minutes until they start floating. Take a colander and put watercress in it. The watercress is wilted when you drain gnocchi over it.
5. Stir in the watercress and drained gnocchi to the pan. Mix everything well. Sprinkle with parmesan and serve immediately.

Homemade Pizza with Tomatoes & Pesto

Dazzle your guest today by baking your own pizza at home with tomatoes, pesto and feta in just 20 minutes

Serves 4

Cooking Time 20 minutes

Nutritional Information: Calories 431, Total Fat 17g, Protein 16g, Carbohydrates 48g, Dietary Fiber 3g

Ingredients

Feta cheese, crumbled -1/2 cup

4 plum tomatoes, sliced

Prepared pesto-1/2 cup

Prepared whole wheat pizza dough-1 pound

Freshly ground pepper

Fresh basil leaves, torn-1/4 cup

Cooking Method

1. Prepare grill to high. Flour a baking sheet.
2. Divide pizza dough into four pieces and roll out each piece into 8-inches circular crust. The thickness of the crust should be ¼ inches. Arrange these crusts on the baking sheet.
3. Grill the pizza crusts for 4 minutes until browned and lightly puffed. Flip the crusts when one side is cooked.
4. Sprinkle immediately with pesto, feta, tomatoes and pepper. Grill for another 4 minutes until lightly browned and the cheese melts. Top with torn basil leaves and serve.

Baked Roasted Green Peppers

Grilled Green peppers stuffed with a mixture of feta, spinach and couscous and baked to perfection

Serves 6

Cooking Time 30 minutes

Nutritional Information: Calories 215, Total Fat 7.6g, Protein 8.7g, Carbohydrates 29g, Dietary Fiber 4g

Ingredients

Cooked couscous -2 cups

Fresh spinach-6 ounces

Lemon juice-1 tablespoon

6 large green bell peppers

4 garlic cloves, minced

Olive oil-1 tablespoon

Salt-1 teaspoon

Feta cheese, crumbled -1/2 cup

Cooking Method

1. Roast green bell peppers for 3 minutes on an open flame until blackened. Use tongs to turn them on the flame.
2. Cover the roasted peppers with plastic wrap and allow them to cool. Remove the plastic wrap and peel the peppers carefully. Cut the top stem with a knife and remove all the seeds. Keep aside.
3. Heat a saucepan coated with cooking oil over medium-high heat. Add garlic and sauté for 1 minute until golden.
4. Reduce heat; stir in spinach and cook for 2 minutes until spinach wilts. Remove from heat. Add salt and lemon juice; Transfer spinach to a bowl. Prepare oven at 350°.
5. Add feta cheese and wilted spinach to the cooked couscous and mix everything well. Stuff this mixture into roasted peeled bell peppers. Place the peppers on a baking sheet lined with aluminium foil.
6. Bake for 8-10 minutes and serve immediately.

Crisp Lettuce Wraps with Red Pepper Hummus

Amazingly bright lettuce wraps stuffed with crunchy veggies inside and served with red pepper hummus

Serves 4

Cooking Time 20 minutes

Nutritional Information: Calories 158, Total Fat 8g, Protein 11.2g, Carbohydrates 12g, Dietary Fiber 3g

Ingredients

Lean ground lamb-6 ounces

Freshly ground black pepper-1/4 teaspoon

Ground cinnamon-1 teaspoon

Canola oil-2 teaspoons

Fresh garlic, minced -2 teaspoons

Chopped onion -1 cup

Toasted pine nuts- 1 tablespoon

Fresh parsley, chopped -1/2 cup

Chopped cucumber -1/2 cup

8 Boston lettuce leaves

Chopped tomato -1/2 cup

Red pepper hummus -1/4 cup

Fat-free Greek yogurt -1/4 cup

Cooking Method

1. Coat a skillet with oil over medium heat. Stir in onion, garlic, cinnamon and sauté for 2 minutes. Add lamb, salt and pepper and cook for 7 minutes until cooked.
2. Combine cucumber, parsley, lam mixture and tomato in a bowl. Mix hummus with yogurt in a separate bowl. Spread the meat mixture on each lettuce leaf. Top with one tablespoon of hummus yoghurt mixture and pine nuts. Seal the wraps with a toothpick.

Halibut Grill with Skordalia

Savory halibut served with grilled veggies and traditional mediterranean garlic potato mash (skordalia)

Serves 4

Cooking Time 30 minutes

Nutritional Information: Calories 387, Total Fat 13g, Protein 30g, Carbohydrates 35g, Dietary Fiber 4g

Ingredients

Zucchini-1 pound

2 red bell peppers, quartered

Halibut fillets-1 pound

Dried thyme-1/4 teaspoon

Plain Greek low-fat yogurt-1/4 cup

1 slice sourdough bread, crust removed

Russet potatoes-1 pound

8 garlic cloves, peeled

Zest and juice of 1 lemon

Salt, divided-1/2 teaspoon

Olive oil, divided-3 tablespoons

1/2 red onion, sliced

Cooking Method

1. Cut zucchini diagonally into 1 inch pieces. Cut halibut into 4 pieces. Peel off potatoes and cut into 1 inch pieces.
2. Put Potatoes and garlic into a saucepan filled with water and cook for 15 minutes over medium-high heat until tender.
3. Meanwhile cut bread into 4 pieces and put in a bowl. Take out 2 tablespoon of cooking water from potatoes and out in the bowl of bread.
4. Stir in olive oil, lemon zest, lemon juice and yoghurt and stir with a spoon to form a smooth paste.
5. After potatoes are cooked, drain in a colander and reserve the liquid in a large bowl. Transfer garlic and potatoes into the bowl of bread mixture.
6. Mash everything well by adding reserved cooking liquid 2 tablespoon at a time. Keep adding reserved liquid until the mixture obtains a desired consistency.
7. Add olive oil and salt; mix and keep it aside.
8. Meanwhile prepare grill over high heat. Drizzle halibut fillets with half teaspoon oil

and season with half teaspoon thyme and salt.

9. Grill fish for 2-3 minutes. Flip and cook the other side too. Flake fish with a skewer to check it. Transfer the fish onto a plate and cover with another plate.
10. Place zucchini, red onion and bell pepper in a bowl. Pour half teaspoon of olive oil and toss. Grill bell pepper in the grill pan over medium heat for 5 minutes. Similarly grill onion and zucchini for 10 minutes and remove when tender.
11. Serve bell pepper, zucchini and onions with the potato mash and grilled fillets.

Authentic Middle Eastern Chicken Shawarma

A Middle Eastern dish of shawarma in which chicken slices dipped in a yoghurt sauce are served in pita pockets

Serves 4

Cooking Time 15 minutes

Nutritional Information: Calories 401, Total Fat 9.8g, Protein 35g, Carbohydrates 39g, Dietary Fiber 2g

Ingredients

4 (6-inch) pitas, halved

1 pound skinless, boneless chicken breast halves, thinly sliced

Fresh parsley, finely chopped -2 tablespoons

Salt-1/2 teaspoon

Plain low-fat Greek-style yogurt-5 tablespoons

Tahini-1 tablespoon

3 garlic cloves, minced and divided

Red pepper, crushed -1/2 teaspoon

Ground coriander-1/8 teaspoon

Ground cumin-1/4 teaspoon

Ground ginger-1/4 teaspoon

Lemon juice, divided-2 tablespoons

Extra-virgin olive oil-2 tablespoons

Chopped red onion-1/4 cup

Chopped plum tomato-1/2 cup

Chopped cucumber -1/2 cup

Cooking Method

1. Combine parsley, salt, red pepper, ginger, cumin and coriander in a bowl. Add in one tablespoon of yoghurt and lemon juice. Beat this mixture with spoon.
2. Now add 2 minced garlic cloves and chicken pieces. Mix so that the chicken is well coated in the yoghurt mixture.
3. Heat olive oil in a skillet over high heat. Add in chicken mixture to skillet; sauté for 7-8 minutes until browned.
4. Combine one fourth cup yoghurt, remaining lemon juice, tahini and garlic in a medium bowl. Place pita halves on the working surface and spread tahini mixture on the inside. Spoon cooked chicken mixture inside pita pockets.
5. Complete pita pockets with 1 tablespoon of tomato, onion and cucumber.

Luscious Fish with Lemon-Fennel Salad

Full of flavour and luscious Halibut Fillets served with lemon fennel salad

Serves 4

Cooking Time 15 minutes

Nutritional Information: Calories 258, Total Fat 9.6g, Protein 36g, Carbohydrates 5.1g, Dietary Fiber 1.6g

Ingredients

Fresh thyme leaves-1 teaspoon

Flat-leaf parsley, chopped -1 tablespoon

Lemon juice-2 tablespoons

Ground coriander-1 teaspoon

Fennel bulb-1 medium

Halibut fillets-4 (6-ounce)

Salt-1/2 teaspoon

Ground cumin-1/2 teaspoon

Freshly ground black pepper-1/4 teaspoon

Extra-virgin olive oil, divided-5 teaspoons

2 garlic cloves, minced

Red onion, thinly sliced -1/4 cup

Cooking Method

1. Cut the fennel bulb into thin slices. Combine coriander, salt, cumin and black pepper in a bowl.
2. Take out one and a half teaspoon spice mixture and mix with garlic and two teaspoons oil in a bowl. Rub this mixture over halibut fillets.
3. Cook the fillets for 5 minutes in a nonstick pan coated with oil over medium heat. Turn and cook the other side too.
4. To the remaining spice mixture, add fennel bulb, oil, parsley, thyme and red onion in a bowl. Toss well to coat
5. Serve fennel salad with cooked fish.

Stuffed Portobello Mushrooms

A traditional stuffed mushroom dish made with mediterranean style stuffing

Serves 4

Cooking Time 30 minutes

Nutritional Information: Calories 181, Total Fat 6.4g, Protein 10g, Carbohydrates 20g, Dietary Fiber 4g

Ingredients

Mixed salad greens-4 cups

Feta cheese, crumbled-1/2 cup

4 portobello caps (4-inch)-3/4 pounds

French bread, toasted-3 cups

Onion, chopped-1/3 cup

Low-fat balsamic vinaigrette-3 tablespoons

Vegetable broth-1/2 cup

Celery, chopped -1/3 cup

Italian seasoning-1/4 teaspoon

Carrot, chopped-1/3 cup

Minced garlic cloves-2

Red bell pepper, chopped -1/4 cup

Cooking spray

Black pepper

Green bell pepper, chopped -1/4 cup

Parmesan cheese, grated-4 teaspoons

Cooking Method

1. Prepare oven at 350°.
2. Clean mushrooms and remove its stems. Chop the stems finely measuring ¼ cup. Combine the chopped stems with onion, celery, carrot, and minced garlic.
3. Coat a nonstick skillet with cooking oil and place it over medium-high heat. Stir in mushroom and onion mixture and cook for 10 minutes until vegetables turns soft & tender. Remove from heat.
4. Combine bread and mushroom onion mixture in a bowl. Toss well to combine. Add vegetable broth gradually to the bread mixture. Add feta and toss gently.
5. Discard brown gills of the mushroom with the help of a spoon. Now arrange these mushrooms on a greased baking sheet with the stem side up.
6. Brush vinaigrette on the mushrooms evenly. Sprinkle with black pepper and parmesan. Top each mushroom with half cup bread mushroom mixture. Bake for 20-22 minutes at 350° until mushroom turns tender.

7. Mix remaining vinaigrette with greens. Divide greens equally on 4 plates and top with one mushroom.

Seasoned Beef Patties and Cucumber Salad

Serve these Beef Patties seasoned with fresh herbs and spices with cucumber salad

Serves 4

Cooking Time 15 minutes

Nutritional Information: Calories 320, Total Fat 11g, Protein 26g, Carbohydrates 21g, Dietary Fiber 1.7g

Ingredients

2 (6-inch) pitas, quartered

Plain fat-free Greek yogurt -1/2 cup

Lemon juice-1 tablespoon

Rice vinegar-2 tablespoons

Ground cinnamon-1/2 teaspoon

English cucumber, thinly sliced -2 cups

Ground cumin-1 teaspoon

Ground coriander-2 teaspoons

Fresh ginger, peeled & chopped -1 tablespoon

Fresh cilantro, chopped -1/4 cup

Cooking spray

Fresh parsley, chopped -1/2 cup

Ground sirloin -1 pound

Salt-1/2 teaspoon

Freshly ground black pepper-1/2 teaspoon

Cooking Method

1. Prepare a grill over medium heat. Spray cooking oil on the prepared grill.
2. In a large bowl, combine meat, half parsley, ginger, cilantro, coriander, cumin, cinnamon and salt
3. Divide the beef mixture equally into 4 portions and make each potion into half inch thick patty. Heat oil in a nonstick pan over medium heat and cook both sides of the patties for 3-3 minutes.
4. Combine vinegar and cucumber in a bowl and toss well.
5. Make yoghurt sauce by combining yoghurt, lemon juice, pepper and 2 tablespoon of chopped parsley in a bowl.
6. Serve 1 patty and half cup cucumber-vinegar mixture on 4 serving plates. Top each patty with two tablespoons of yogurt sauce.
7. Serve patties with pita wedges.

Turkey with Honeyed Grapefruit Relish

Fresh tasting relish provides a contrast to the spiced turkey

Serves 2

Cooking Time: 30 minutes

Nutritional Information: Calories 337, Total Fat 15g, Protein 32g, Carbohydrates 22g, Dietary Fiber 6g

Ingredients

Avocado-grapefruit Relish

1 large grapefruit, seedless

Honey-1 teaspoon

Red-wine vinegar-1 teaspoon

1 small shallot, minced

1/2 avocado, diced

Fresh cilantro, chopped -1 tablespoon

Spiced turkey

2 turkey cutlets- 8 ounces

Five-spice powder-1/2 teaspoon

Chili powder-1 tablespoon

Canola oil-1 tablespoon

Cooking Method

1. For relish: Take a sharp knife and peel off the grapefruit and remove the white pith. Squeeze out the juice from grapefruit's segments in a bowl. Add shallot, avocado, honey, vinegar and cilantro. Combine everything.
2. For turkey: Mix five-spice powder, salt and chili powder in a bowl. Rub this mixture over turkey pieces.
3. Cook turkey in a nonstick skillet for 3 minutes over medium heat. Serve with grapefruit-avocado relish.

Spicy Chicken Thighs in Brussels sprouts

Paprika rubbed chicken thighs nestled into shallots and Brussels sprouts

Serves 4

Cooking Time: 30 minutes

Nutritional Information: Calories 440, Total Fat 26g, Protein 42g, Carbohydrates 14g, Dietary Fiber 5g

Ingredients

4 large chicken thighs, bone-in - 2 1/2 pounds

Brussels sprouts-1 pound

Dried thyme-1 teaspoon

Sweet paprika, smoked -1 tablespoon

Garlic, minced-2 cloves

4 small shallots, quartered

Ground pepper, divided-1/2 teaspoon

1 lemon, sliced

Salt, divided-3/4 teaspoon

Extra-virgin olive oil, divided-3 tablespoons

Cooking Method

1. Trim Brussels sprouts and cut into halves. Combine shallots, lemon and Brussels sprouts, one-fourth teaspoon salt, pepper and two tablespoons oil in a bowl. Spread this mixture over a rimmed baking sheet.
2. Now mash minced garlic with half teaspoon salt, thyme, paprika, pepper and one tablespoon oil in a bowl. Spread this paste over chicken pieces. Nestle chicken thighs into Brussels sprouts.
3. Preheat oven to 450°F and place rack in the lower third.
4. Roast the chicken in the preheated oven for 20 minutes until done.

Lemon-Mint Parsley Tabbouleh

A fresh parsley salad with a toss of cucumber, tomatoes and bulgur

Serves 4

Cooking Time: 30 minutes

Nutritional Information: Calories 166, Total Fat 7.6g, Protein 4.3g, Carbohydrates 21, Dietary Fiber 5g

Ingredients

4 scallions, thinly sliced

1 small cucumber, diced

2 tomatoes, diced

Water-1 cup

Fresh mint, chopped -1/4 cup

Bulgur-1/2 cup

Lemon juice-1/4 cup

Extra-virgin olive oil-2 tablespoons

Freshly ground pepper, to taste

Minced garlic-1/2 teaspoon

Flat-leaf parsley, finely chopped - 2 cups

Salt-1/4 teaspoon

Cooking Method

1. Take bulgur with 1 cup water in a saucepan and boil. After a boil, cover and remove from heat.
2. Let stand for 20 minutes until the bulgur absorbs the water fully and is tender. Drain and keep aside to cool.
3. In a bowl; make a dressing by combining oil, pepper, salt garlic and lemon juice.
4. To bulgur, add scallions, cucumber, mint, tomatoes and parsley. Pour the dressing over the bulgur and toss.
5. Serve immediately or refrigerate before serving.

Herb Crusted Lamb Chops with Couscous Salad

A tasty mediterranean herb crusted lamb chops dish served with couscous salad

Serves 4

Cooking Time: 30 minutes

Nutritional Information: Calories 331, Total Fat 15g, Protein 34g, Carbohydrates 17g, Dietary Fiber 3g

Ingredients

Whole-wheat couscous-1/2 cup

8 lamb loin chops-2 1/2 pounds

Crumbled feta-1/2 cup

Water-1 cup

Lemon juice-3 tablespoons

Minced garlic-1 tablespoon

2 tomatoes, chopped

Fresh parsley, chopped -1 tablespoon

Salt-1/4 teaspoon

Extra-virgin olive oil-2 teaspoons

1 cucumber, chopped

Fresh dill, finely chopped -2 tablespoons

Cooking Method

1. In a bowl, combine parsley, garlic and salt. Rub this parsley-garlic mixture over lamb chops, covering all sides.
2. Meanwhile heat olive oil in a nonstick pan over medium heat and cook both sides lamb chops for 6-6 minutes until done. Keep it warm.
3. Boil 1 cup water in a saucepan. Add in couscous and return to heat. Cover and let simmer for 3 minutes.
4. Let stand the couscous 4 minutes and fluff with a fork. Place couscous in a bowl and add in cucumber, tomatoes, dill, lemon juice and feta.
5. Mix well and serve it with cooked lamb chops.

Grouper Fillets in a Tomato-Caper Sauce

Fish simmering in a richly flavored sauce of tomatoes and capers

Serves 4

Cooking Time:

Nutritional Information: Calories 216, Total Fat 6.5g, Protein 30g, Carbohydrates 8.6g, Dietary Fiber 2.3g

Ingredients

1 julienne cut jalapeno chili (1-inch)

Capers, rinsed-1 tablespoon

5 large green olives (pimiento-stuffed), sliced

4 grouper fillets (1-inch thick & 5 ounces)

3 tomatoes, diced

Lime juice-2 tablespoons

2 cloves garlic, minced

1 yellow onion, finely chopped

Freshly ground black pepper-1/4 teaspoon

Olive oil-1 1/2 tablespoons

Cooking Method

1. Sprinkle grouper fillets with pepper and salt. Heat oil in a saucepan over medium heat. Stir in fish and cook both sides of the fish for 3 minutes until browned. Keep warm.
2. Add one tablespoon of oil to the same pan and add onion. Sauté for minutes until soft. Stir in garlic and cook for 1 minute.
3. Now add diced tomatoes, jalapeno, capers and olives and let simmer for a couple of minutes. After the flavors blend in, add pepper and salt to taste.
4. Add fish to other ingredients in the pan. Cover with a lid and let simmer for 6 minutes until the fish is opaque in the center.
5. Place fillets onto serving plates. Pour lime juice into the pan of vegetables and stir it once. Spoon vegetables and sauce over each fillet and serve immediately.

Sautéed Vegetable Calzone

A calzone stuffed with sautéed vegetables, tomato slices and cheese

Serves 2

Cooking Time:

Nutritional Information: Calories 253, Total Fat 8g, Protein 11g, Carbohydrates 33g, Dietary Fiber 4g

Ingredients

Pizza sauce-2/3 cup

Mozzarella cheese, shredded-1/2 cup

1 medium tomato, sliced

Asparagus stalks-3

Whole-wheat bread dough loaf-1/2 pound

Spinach, chopped -1/2 cup

Olive oil-2 teaspoons

Sliced mushrooms-1/2 cup

Minced garlic-2 tablespoons

Chopped broccoli-1/2 cup

Cooking Method

1. Cut asparagus into pieces of 1-inch. Prepare oven at 400°F. Grease a large baking sheet.
2. Combine together spinach, asparagus, mushrooms, garlic, broccoli and one teaspoon of oil in a bowl. Sauté the vegetable for 4 minutes in a nonstick saucepan.
3. Divide bread dough into two halves and roll out each half into an oval shape with the rolling pin.
4. Spoon half of the sautéed vegetables, tomato slices on each of the rolled dough. Sprinkle with cheese. Fold over and seal the edges by pressing it.
5. Brush oil over calzones and place on the greased baking sheet. Bake for 2 minutes until calzones turns golden brown. Heat pizza sauce inside a microwave. Serve calzone with pizza sauce.

Savory Poached Pears

Poached pear is an incredibly tasty option for weeknight desserts

Serves 4

Cooking Time: 30 minutes

Nutritional Information: Calories 134, Total Fat 0.6g, Protein 1g, Carbohydrates 33g, Dietary Fiber 2g

Ingredients

Orange zest-2 tablespoons

Orange juice-One cup

4 whole pears

Apple juice-1/3 cup

Ground cinnamon-2 teaspoon

Fresh raspberries-Half cup

Ground nutmeg-1 teaspoon

Cooking Method

1. Combine orange juice, apple juice, nutmeg and cinnamon in a bowl.
2. Peel off 4 whole pears leaving the stems. Take out core from pear's bottom and add the pears in a nonstick pan.
3. Stir in the orange-apple juice mix from bowl and reduce the heat to medium. Let simmer for 30 minutes. Turn pears frequently.
4. Place pears onto serving plates and garnish with orange zest. Serve immediately.

Icy Almond Date Yoghurt Shake

A thick creamy ice cold almond date shake with yoghurt and nutmeg dusting

Serves 4

Cooking Time: 10 minutes

Nutritional Information: Calories 141, Total Fat 2g, Protein 3g, Carbohydrates 28g, Dietary Fiber 2g

Ingredients

Ground nutmeg-1/4 teaspoon

Pitted dates, chopped -1/3 cup

Warm water-3 tablespoons

Chilled almond milk -2 cups

4 ice cubes

Dairy yogurt-1/2 cup

1 very ripe banana, frozen

Cooking Method

1. Sprinkle 2 tablespoon of warm water over dates inside a bowl and allowed it to soak for 4 minutes. Drain.
2. Blend dates, banana, yoghurt, almond milk in a blender and transfer the mix to a bowl.
3. Blend ice cubes too in a blender.
4. Take tall glasses and place crushed ice cubes at the bottom. Fill the glass with banana-date mixture. Dust nutmeg on top.
5. Serve chilled.

Braised Garlic Kale with Cherry Tomatoes

Savory kale made with cherry tomatoes and garlic

Serves 4

Cooking Time:

Nutritional Information: Calories 92, Total Fat 3g, Protein 4.5g, Carbohydrates 16g, Dietary Fiber 3g

Ingredients

Extra-virgin olive oil-2 teaspoons

4 garlic cloves, thinly sliced

Vegetable broth-1/2 cup

Fresh lemon juice-1 tablespoon

Cherry tomatoes, halved-1 cup

Salt-1/4 teaspoon

Kale-1 pound

Freshly ground black pepper-1/8 teaspoon

Cooking Method

1. Take kale and remove its tough stems. Chop the leaves coarsely
2. Heat olive oil in a frying pan over medium heat.
3. Add in garlic slices; sauté for 2 minutes until lightly browned. Add kale and cook for 1-2 minutes. Add vegetable stock; reduce heat to low and cover with a lid. Cook for 5 minutes until kale wilts
4. Add cherry tomatoes and cook for 7 minutes until the vegetables are tender.
5. Take the pan from heat. Add in lemon juice and season with pepper and salt. Serve immediately.

Traditional Lentil & Bulgur Pilaf with Squash

A terrific pilaf prepared in a traditional way with lentils, bulgur and squash

Serves 6

Cooking Time: 30 minutes

Nutritional Information: Calories 256, Total Fat 3g, Protein 15g, Carbohydrates 41g, Dietary Fiber 12g

Ingredients

Vegetable broth-4 1/2 cups

1 bay leaf

Brown lentils, rinsed-1 1/4 cups

Salt, or to taste-1/4 teaspoon

Coarse bulgur- 3/4 cup

Ground allspice-1/2 teaspoon

Freshly ground pepper, to taste

Lemon juice-2 tablespoons

1 small yellow squash,

Extra-virgin olive oil-1 tablespoon

1 small zucchini

Freshly grated lemon zest-2 teaspoons

1 clove garlic, minced

Fresh parsley, chopped -2 tablespoons

1 medium onion, chopped

Fresh cilantro, chopped -2 tablespoons

Cooking Method

1. Cut zucchini and squash into two halves lengthwise and then cut into ¼ inch slices.
2. Combine lentils, onion, broth, bay leaf, allspice, pepper and salt in a saucepan over medium-high heat. After a boil, reduce the heat ,
3. Cover with a lid and cook for 15-18 minutes. Stir in bulgur. Cook for 15 minutes until the liquid is fully absorbed and lentils are tender.
4. Remove from heat. Take out bay leaf and pour lemon juice.
5. Heat oil in a skillet and add squash and zucchini over medium heat. Stir in garlic along with lemon zest and sauté for 3 minutes.
6. Add cilantro, parsley and pepper and stir with a spatula. Serve hot with whole wheat pita.

Beef Rice Bake with Mushrooms & Cranberries

Delicious and quick brown rice bake with beef, mushrooms and cranberries

Serves 6

Cooking Time:

Nutritional Information: Calories 506, Total Fat 9g, Protein 50g, Carbohydrates 51g, Dietary Fiber 3.2g

Ingredients

Cooked brown rice-3 cups

Ground turkey-2 pounds

1 onion, chopped

5 garlic cloves, minced

1 green bell pepper, sliced

Baby Bella mushrooms, sliced-2 cups

Italian dried herbs – rosemary, fennel, thyme, oregano, basil

Nutmeg

Paprika

Fire roasted tomatoes, crushed -1 14-0z can

Balsamic vinegar-2-3 tablespoons

Whole cranberries-3/4 cup

Kalamata black olives, chopped-1/2 cup

Rinsed capers-2 tablespoons

Fresh parsley, chopped-1/2 cup

Sea salt

Fresh grounded pepper

Extra virgin olive oil-5 tablespoon

Cooking Method

1. Heat a skillet coated with olive oil over medium-high heat. Add onions and garlic; sauté for 2 minutes. Stir in turkey, mushrooms and peppers and cook for 8 minutes.
2. Now season with dried herbs- oregano, basil, rosemary, fennel and thyme. Add in spices, tomatoes, olives, parsley, capers, cranberries and balsamic vinegar. Stir well with a spatula. Season with pepper and salt to taste.
3. Preheat oven to 350ºF. Grease a baking dish (lasagna-style) lightly with cooking oil. Spread brown rice at the bottom evenly with a spoon
4. Drizzle 1 tablespoon of olive oil over rice and fluff with a fork. Season with ground pepper and sea salt.
5. Add turkey mixture over rice and spread with a spatula. Sprinkle with crumbled feta on top. Drizzle olive oil over turkey for a kick.
6. Cover with a foil. Bake for 30 minutes until done.

Purple Cabbage and Sunflower Butter Soup

A nutritious bright purple cabbage soup with sunflower seed butter

Serves 4

Cooking Time: 30 minutes

Nutritional Information: Calories 590, Total Fat 31g, Protein 15g, Carbohydrates 68g, Dietary Fiber 2g

Ingredients

Olive oil-2 tablespoons

Hot Thai Kitchen curry paste-1 1/2 teaspoons

1 red onion, diced

4-5 cloves garlic, minced

1 sweet potato, diced

Shredded purple cabbage-1/2 head

Yellow pepper, chopped -1 cup

Vegetable broth-3 cups

Sunflower seed butter, melted-1/2 cup

Coconut milk-1 14-oz. can

Red pepper flakes, crushed-1/4 teaspoon

Fresh cilantro, chopped -2-3 tablespoons

1 lime juice

Agave nectar-1 tablespoon

Salt and pepper

Cooking Method

1. Heat olive oil in a large pot. Stir in curry paste and sauté for 30 seconds until the spice is infused with the oil.
2. Add in garlic, onion, yellow pepper, cabbage and sweet potato.
3. Stir continuously and cook for 5 minutes until vegetables are soft.
4. Pour broth, coconut milk. Then add sunflower butter, cilantro and red pepper flakes. Cover and let the soup simmer for 25 minutes until vegetables are soft and tender.
5. Add lime juice at the end and adjust its seasoning. Add organic brown sugar or agave to balance heat.
6. Garnish with chopped cilantro.

Basil walnut Pesto Spread

A yummy pesto sauce made with fresh basil leaves and walnuts in minutes

Serves-4

Cooking Time: 10 Minutes

Nutritional Information: Calories 86, Total Fat 9g, Protein 3g, Carbohydrates 2g, Dietary Fiber 0.5g

Ingredients

3 cups fresh basil leaves

2 garlic cloves

Walnuts-1/2 cup

Extra virgin olive oil, fruity -10 tablespoons

Grated Parmesan-1/2 cup

Sea salt

Cooking Method

1. Remove the stems of basil leaves. Wash and pat to dry.
2. Put all the ingredients together in a food processor and process to form a smooth paste. Adjust the seasoning.
3. Serve immediately as an appetizer. Spread it on flatbread or artichoke hearts.
4. You can refrigerate it if you want to eat it later. Coat with a layer of olive oil; keep inside an air tight container and refrigerate.

Conclusion

This delectable recipe book presents traditional dishes from all over the Mediterranean region. This recipe book is a super addition to anyone's cookbook shelf. The book takes a tour through the region: meat loaves with arugula salad from Greece, eggplant dip from Turkey, grilled vegetable tagine from Morocco and lemon-mint parsley tabbouleh from Lebanon.

The Mediterranean diet has been scientifically proven to reduce the risk of a number of diseases including cancer and heart stroke. It's a wonderful resource for families that want to stay healthy without compromising on taste.

The robust flavors are perfect for summer entertaining. Throw a party for your friends. The quick & easy Mediterranean diet cookbook will give your guests an exquisite experience of sunny Mediterranean and your guests will be begging you for the secret recipe.